ALL THAT GLITTERS

STEFANO DE ROSSI

This book is dedicated to my editor, who is about to realize just how little of her input I used.

CONTENTS

LIFE

THERE ARE RULES, MY DEAR

There are rules in this house, my dear
First person up makes coffee
Not a single cup
But enough for whoever is still in bed
They especially do not drink it all for themselves
Nor do they simply 'forget' to prep another
Your excuses are bullshit
You shall be hearing from my lawyer

A RAINY DAY

The rain splutters on the pavement outside
Kicked into a heavy mist from cars driving by
The unending gray skies and distant rumble
Hurrying walkers along as they fight the bite in the air
Drizzle across every forehead
And fat drops clinging to the leaves all around
That petrichor whenever the clouds fall
Now with a whine from a plane slowing on its descent
A cool afternoon with the lights on
Curled up on a sofa
With a fluffball twitching beside my feet
A coffee-lined thick-handled mug nearby
And a book of escapism keeping me there
I can't help but smell the pages
Transported into a world of book shops and fantasy
Where the quiet can retreat from the frantic outdoors
At peace under the rumbling skies
And in total bliss among the pages

STUNNING

She was stunning
A simple crush over the years
With a smile that melted me
And curves that crippled my mind
I was hardly the only one
Who couldn't think straight when she was around
Always hoping that one day
She would look at me with a new curiosity in her eye
A longing
Willing to take a chance
But it never came
Instead we bonded
Always moving around
Yet always catching up when we could
Pained whenever life hit the other too hard
Giving me a safe place to talk through agony
Giving her a chance to put into words all that crippled her
Laughing at stupid jokes
And reminiscing about how we used to be
One day it came
I found the crush had faded
And had been for some time
I don't miss the what-could-have-been
For it was never meant to be

And living her life even second-hand was sobering
Perhaps not just sobering but harrowing
One day she acknowledged how I used to look at her
How everyone used to look at her
And how some still do
Every conversation was filler
Hoping to find the right combination of words
To see what was beneath that dress
Under those jeans
Behind that bra
Some found ways, of course
Some plied her with alcohol
Others found a way to see her
When they thought she didn't know
Some ...
Sometimes she fought the misery
By seeking their attention
Sometimes she retreated into pills to escape
She has scars on her wrists
From when someone refused to let her go
Abusive texts from those who can't stand being ignored
There are people who follow her home
And pictures of her online
Still, she's fearless

She's seen the bottom of the pit
And has climbed out of it on her own
Travels the world alone because fuck living in fear
She was dealt a winning hand in looks
And has managed to build a winning hand in attitude
She sings and dances and laughs every damn day
And she is stunning
Now more so than before

TRAPPED

I'm trapped
In a cabin-fever madness
Six weeks utterly alone
No one home
No one to talk to
No job
Slowly going insane
My last friend on her way out of the country
Living a life carefree and wild
While I stare into the mirror
Broke
Unable to even fill my car
See new things
Or do anything other than survive
So I wait
Staying awake until eight a.m.
Anxiety so high I refuse to go to bed
Afraid of the endless spiral of doom that awaits
As I toss and turn and give up in a daze
Too poor for wine or vodka
Too poor for anything
Except hanging every hope I have
On random numbers in the lottery
Desperate for a way out

Yet losing half of what I spend every time
Like fate laughs at my hopes for an instant way out
Now an echo of who I used to be
I used to be outgoing
Used to be motivated
Creative
And happy in my solitude
But now I'm unable to see if this will ever end
Questioning reality
As the days bleed from one into the next
Never knowing for sure where I am
How much longer I still have to go
Trapped
With no ray of light to guide me
No touch from another person
No hope of ever getting out of here
The darkness spreading
And little by little
I start to welcome the insanity

OCTOBER

I have no idea where the year has gone
It feels like just last week we rang in January
And now we're closing in on October once again
It was a blur of inactivity
Frustration and boredom
I spent more time doing chores than actually living
I didn't read all the books I should've
Didn't see all the people I meant to
I didn't lose those extra pounds
And I'm pretty sure I put more on instead
Every day has bled into the next
Everything still looks the same
A walk for fresh air along the same roads as before
The takeaway place knows my order without having to ask
I have more gray hairs
And have cooked nothing new
I blinked and a whole month went by
Slept and passed a whole season
And it's getting worse
I can't remember when these wrinkles first came to be
But they remain even when I relax my face
I gasp at the price of things
Because I remember how they much they were
Just a few years ago

Which turns out to be half a life-time ago
I used to travel
Stay the night at friends'
Stumble home with the sun rising in my eyes
And talk drunken bullshit
Beside a fountain in the middle of some city
I'd visit tourist spots and have a burger by the beach
Explore museums and artifacts from war
Make the new cinema release a big event
And spend all day covered in grime
To hear a hundred bands play
Now I can't be bothered
And I can't remember what happened to my last birthday
Did I work or take the day off?
Did we go out or stay in?
It was a busy time at work
So we probably couldn't be bothered leaving the house
When was the last comedy show I saw in person?
Or the last concert I went to?
When did my attention span go from movie marathons
To giving up after five minutes
Because it hasn't grabbed me yet?
Who are these contacts in my phone?
And who is that naive idiot on my old driver's license?

When I go out and say, 'I should do this more often,'
Why don't I actually do this more often?
Why is hiding away at home easier
Than putting on something fresh and going out for coffee?
Is it because I have coffee at home?
Or because there's always that one annoying person
Wherever you go?
When did life become an endless series of chores?
And where are these roses I should be smelling?
Anyway
I have an incomplete board game on the table
That needs to be packed up
A stack of dishes I should probably wash
And a lawn to mow
Maybe I should text someone to see how they are
And organize to meet up soon
Not this month because I'm busy
But October definitely
Certainly before the end of the year
Because I miss them
At least, I think I miss them
And if I don't miss them
I definitely miss the old me
Even if my life is technically better

With a mortgage instead of roommates
A decent bed instead of a mattress on the floor
I don't miss the anxiety
But I do miss the adventure
Where every year was something new
Instead of every year disappearing
With tomorrow being the same
As it was today

GET OFF MY LAWN

I didn't expect old age to start so soon
But here we are
I saw my parents turn forty
My dad completely gray with thinned hair
My mom double chinned and wrinkles formed
My grandparents wheezing whenever they sat
Snoring whenever they slept
Wearing old man caps and using a walking stick unironically
Working part time after they had retired
Knitting in front of the TV
Hiding the damn thing in a wooden chest with doors
Like no one should know they own a TV
They talked about things so boring and small
About people I've never met and never will
They moved slowly instead of running from house to house
Adults never seemed to have any Lego
And were obsessed with no elbows on the table
They rolled their eyes at the clothes we wanted to buy
And didn't know the biggest celebrities in the world
We spoke the same language but could barely communicate
They'd say stupid things like
"You'll understand when you're older"
That was old age
And now here I am, a few months after forty

My first gray hair at sixteen
Having to dye my hair full time at twenty two
Twisting my knee the same year and it never fully healing
Realizing my music was classic rock before I was thirty
Throwing my back out from sleeping on a shitty mattress
To seeing my high school friends now with teenage kids
Friends divorced
Talking about their mortgages
Some going back to school with those half their age
I have grays on my chest now
Grays down below
My hair isn't just thinning but has thinned
Exercise wipes me out if I skip a single day
I snore almost every night when I didn't just five years before
I have a herb garden I can't keep alive
And I wear an extra layer instead of turning up the heat
Everyone keeps trying to take my money
And I spend it on retro things from my childhood
But the sweets and crisps I used to live on nauseate me now
And I'm exhausted after eighteen hours awake
Music today is god awful
With no soul or point to any of it
Your slang is dumb and is passing me by
I don't know who the popular artists are anymore

And I really don't care
The actors I like are starting to die
Some of them younger than me
Most of cancer
Others to suicide
My heroes as a kid are turning out to be colossal assholes
I pulled a muscle just rolling over in bed
And it took two weeks to heal
I have an entry level job with twenty year olds
Who blow their paycheck on partying, drugs, and booze
They're aghast at how old I am and how we don't relate
And I don't give a single fuck about them
Every boss I have can go suck a dick
And I don't believe the politicians anymore
I couldn't possibly date a twenty five year old
And the milfs I like long for the passion of youth like me
They don't pussy-foot about because time is running out
I sometimes forget which story came from which girlfriend
And I can't remember more than three phone numbers
But it's okay
It happened to me
It'll happen to you
Thankfully teenage angst and social anxiety is gone
Everyone is better at sex at forty than at sixteen

Falling in love with someone new every week was exhausting
And I can eat what I want when I want
My toys are better than your toys
And I know how to take care of things I bought
I don't have to go to school unless I want to
And I no longer stress out about getting good grades
I miss a few things, sure
But not enough to go back

ALONE

I stood in a crowded room
Utterly alone
Wishing there was a cat to stroke
Or something interesting to stare at beyond the road outside
Those gathered were getting drunker by the minute
Yet I had to drive
Wanting my friends to hurry so I could leave
While wondering where they were
As their Mr Hyde's took over
They were intending to stay for beyond six hours
I hoped to be gone after just one
So I waited
A sober soul in a room full of drunks
Listening to them spout pearls of wisdom
Then hitting on each other
Only to then make snide remarks
While bemoaning how dull life was
As they topped up their cup with another drink
Until it dawned on me
I'd been to this exact same party before
In the same house with the same hosts and guests
Four years had passed and everyone was still moaning
Hitting on someone new
Still philosophizing and complaining about others

Still in the same dead-end job
Still working on their Ph.D.

Only now I also had a dead-end job
Complaining about the same bullshit as before
And striking out instead of taking someone home
I was trapped
In a moment where I was truly alone
Watching as everyone sank another drink
Wishing another happy birthday
And that we'll all do it again this time next year

DEAR YOUNGER ME

Dear younger me
Someone close to you is not going to make it
I need you to reach out
I need you to show them that someone cares
Because they are screaming on the inside
While calm on the exterior
And getting dangerously close
To resigned and determined

You might not be able to help them
And it's okay if you can't
But their last day is rapidly approaching
It's coming faster than you can handle
You might not be able to ease their suffering
But there's no harm in trying to make someone smile
Even if that smile is for the very last time

IT NEVER ENDS

After a year and a half I'm still living in a renovation project
We gutted the whole house and plastered it ourselves
Stuffed insulation into the walls
And painted every damn surface
Sanded the floors
Moved walls and doorways
Knocked out the laundry room to expand the kitchen
Ripped up the concrete pathway out the back
And stuffed the debris into the crumbling garage
We're nearly there with the interior
I promise
But we crashed
Utterly
Completely
Crashed
There's paint and plaster splotches all over the floor
Skirting boards missing on every wall
Wires are sticking out of holes
Because we don't have sockets installed
Bulbs hang free because we haven't bought the fixtures yet
Doors absent on rooms because we're too tired to hang them
Not a single kitchen cabinet built
And a cracked stove top
That will cost at least a grand to replace

A paint-splattered sink that is starting to whine
Plates and bowls over there
Yet knives and forks all the way over here
The floor needs to be sanded again
And touch up paint jobs done in every room
Temporary curtains hang over the windows
The backyard is an overgrown mess
There's sealer glue smeared across the windows
A great wall of paint cans stacked outside
Every piece of furniture has been moved too many times
And I can't remember where anything is
Definitely can't find our set of screwdrivers
And why does the drill always need charging?
The cat flap is just a hole in the wall
And we're missing floorboards everywhere we go
Not a single room is finished
And we haven't done a damn thing in six months
We're burnt out
So burnt out that it's easier to live in an incomplete house
Than spend two hours working on a simple project
Because there are now too many simple projects
And it's easier to ignore it all than to tackle one thing at a time
Since knocking off just one thing still leaves a hundred more
And it's never quick

Never perfect
It's barely even good enough
It's good enough for now
And I know we'll have to come back to it
But we don't
And all the errors are starting to haunt me
As is our depleted budget so we can't hire anyone to save us
It wasn't a mistake to try this all ourselves
But we certainly bit off more than we could chew
We're closer to finished than started
And everything else is within our grasp
But it's just easier to spend the weekend watching TV
Than going to the store to argue about paint schemes
And the position of cabinets
It'd be easier if we could agree on how to do things
But we don't
And the bickering about how to do the job is worse
Than doing the job itself
So now I understand the thousand yard stare from others
Who originally thought they could do it all themselves
But we'll be done by Christmas
I promise
Though which Christmas is still up for debate

ALWAYS DIRTY

Why is my house always so dirty?
There's a used mug in a bowl on a plate
Next to a grimy glass of inverted spoons and forks
How?
HOW!?
The kitchen was clean just two hours ago
Tumbleweeds of dust bounce past me in the hallway
When I vacuumed the whole place yesterday
The kitchen counter needs to be wiped down all the time
My still-wearable clothes on the back of the chair
Could be mistaken for Quasimodo
The hamper is full
And what's on the clothes rack has been dry for days
Yet I always seem to be doing laundry
I cleaned my desk just last week
Now there are torn envelopes with lists of reminders on the back
Bills laughing at me as everyone keeps taking away my money
Books I use for reference
Pens tossed about
Notes for stories written while at work
Notes for work written while at home
And cables
How do I have so many damn cables?
And how the hell do they all get magically tangled together?

I mowed the lawn the other day
And now there are a hundred tufts of spiky grass that stab my soles
There's cat hair on the top of every sofa
Cat hair under the bed
And on everything I wear
Muddy paw prints on my windscreen
And their biscuits scattered a mile away from their bowl
The windows are always filthy
And there's incense ash on the table
Crumbs from a sandwich
And a shard of broken glass from god knows where
Are we going to finish this card game from last weekend
Or should I pack it away?
How come I can never find the remote
Even though I leave it in the same place every day?
I swear there's a whole family living here in secret
Mocking me as I clean up after them
Enjoying my efforts when I never can
And don't even get me started on the amount of hair in the shower

HERE WE ARE AGAIN

So here we are
Lamenting over another hangover
My kidneys are stabbing me
My liver is about to burst
And my stomach feels like it's being dissolved in vinegar
Bacon and coffee might ease the sting behind my eyes
But it doesn't help with chastising the idiot last night
It's not that I drank a lot last night
I mean I did
But nothing out of the ordinary
It's that I've drunk a lot this week
And I might do it again today
I didn't expect to last night
But I was feeling good so I had a drink
Though it's never just one
It's always enough to keep the buzz going
And one more to make the journey worth it
Hard and fast
And now I have to be social around people I can't be bothered with
Bored around people I can't stand
So maybe I won't drink a lot
Certainly not enough to make people wonder
My mind over matter should be strong enough
Despite it being a good day when I can keep it to one bottle of wine

And a congratulatory day when it's three quarters
But I've had three bad days in a row now
And another three bad days in a row earlier this week
I don't know what the excuse is anymore
I drink when I'm bored
I drink when in a good mood
I drink when I'm stressed
I drink when I'm social
I drink because she's drinking with me
And I drink because it's there
Three quarters of a bottle used to wipe me out
Slur me to death
Now I function easily on twice that
No one complains
No one sees me slur
No one sees me lose track or my focus
I keep my shit together after a few
And have never needed to apologize for my behavior
Except for that one time
Somehow this has snuck up on me
And I don't know how
It used to be a once a week thing
Now it's twice the quantity and four times as often
Surely I can't be that bored

Tomorrow I'll be better

Tomorrow I'll be good

Because I'm starting to fear that this is the road to Alzheimer's

Diabetes or a stroke

I can't lose my mind later on in life

I simply can't

I can't be a bumbling old fool who drank away his future

So I need to be better

One day

Maybe tomorrow

Because I'm pretty sure it won't be today

WHAT THE HELL IS WRONG WITH YOU?

What the hell is wrong with you?
Why have you been awake for an hour
And still can't get out of bed?
Why are you bursting to go to the bathroom
And still not going?
Why is the pressure on your bladder
The only thing that might make you move?
Go make some coffee and have some food
Not the crap you ate last night but something healthy
Something healthy to get you out of this malaise
Because while you laze here in a daze
There are others going about their day
And they are starting to see through your charade
You can't call in sick again because you've done it too often
You can't call on your friends again
Because you have nothing new to tell them
And even pretending that you're okay
Burns you out completely
And you need all the energy you can muster
To get your ass to work
So just get out of bed and do something meaningful
And have a shower while you're at it
You can't feel good if you're caked in BO
Don't check the news because it's always dire

I said don't check the news because it's always–
Fine, look for that ray of light in a world of decay
Scroll through those motivational posts
Supposedly written by Marilyn Monroe
Go to the gym and do some cardio
No, that means having to go out in public
And you can't deal with that right now
And you definitely can't perform your best
With day-old frozen pizza for breakfast
Have some oats and berries
Or that green smoothie recipe you saved a month ago
Or three months ago, as it turns out
But first you need to go shopping and deal with the crowds
Better just grab something from the gas station
On your way to work
And hope to remember to buy something green
On your way back
Put on some fresh socks and underwear because it'll feel good
And not the three day old t-shirt because the hamper's full
And you can't be bothered doing a load
Wash all the dishes because the clutter still overwhelms you
And put on some music instead of sitting in silence
Go for a walk and see a tree
Then lift some weights until you're the perfect you

Start small and build a routine
Write an affirmation you actually believe in
Reach out to a friend even though it'll tire you out
Ask how they're doing
Maybe they might make you laugh
Despite not having genuinely smiled in weeks
And hope they answer when you call
Because you don't have the energy to be 'on'
If they call you back later
But first you need to get out of bed
Go to work and pretend to mean it when you say you're fine
It's not rocket science, you know what to do
So why can't you remember to do any of it?
Why is motivation even an issue?
Just go and do it
Do it right now
Just put your phone away
And get out of bed

MY WILD FRIEND

My friend is at the wheel again
Deciding where to go
What to do
Down another strange road
Impatient at everyone in our way
And determined to get us into all kinds of trouble
In the name of fun and adventure
I know I shouldn't
I know I risk burning every bridge I've ever built
But what can I do?
His exhilaration draws me in
And little by little I start to feel alive
For he's at the wheel again
Deciding where we go
And what we do

Now the sludge of despair is my companion
Ruin abounds
And friends ashamed to know me
But see, he was the one in control, not me
Please understand
We may have the same memories
But make none of the same choices
He faces none of the consequences

While I face them all
That when he's in town
No amount of vodka will keep him down
Sleep is unnecessary
And no one else can keep up
It's a party for one and all
Where I'm both host and guest of honor
Where burying my face in my girlfriend's tits is oh so boring
When I could nuzzle up in anyone else's
Doesn't matter whose
But hers over there look quite enchanting
Even though there's a quiet voice screaming inside
My friend glides us over to her
Ready to try his luck
Where every friend in my phone is a hook-up waiting to be
And the stranger we just met
Proves that soul mates truly exist
That the gods of destiny are shining the way
And the euphoria of finding your one true love like this
Is why my friend exists in the first place
When old hobbies disappear and the new take hold
The old you hoping for something quiet like water colours
While maybe curious about the life
Of being a borderless photographer

Which matters not a damn
Because his idea of fun is black diamond mountain biking
No matter your age
Or skill
And holy shit the rush of it all sounds perfect
Then we'll go to a shooting range
To help blow off some steam
And when we're done we'll order everything off the menu
Withdraw a thousand dollars and head to the casino
Go on a road trip
Or fly anywhere else
Fuck it – let's fly there now
Jump on the next plane out of here and be somewhere new
Be the adventurer I crave to be
Meet whoever looks fun in a beachside bar
And spend a perfect day with them
Then fly back before anyone realizes I was gone
Because challenges are meant to be conquered
And by god today is that day when I grab life by the horns
Finally living to my full potential
My heart racing with discovery
And energy crackling through every inch of my skin
Where every mysterious sign is telling me to go for it
And work can shove it because it's not a forever job anyway

And they need me more than I need them
So here are my demands
And if I don't get a raise on the spot
Then they can kiss my ass goodbye
Because for the first time in two years I feel alive once again

My friend is driving
And while everyone says they sort of understand
They don't get why I can't help to navigate
Because surely I'm still inside
Aware of the consequences and able to say no
That even though we arrive somewhere new
I don't need to go along with him
Or that if I recognize the symptoms while still at home
Why I don't ask for help
Because if this has the power to ruin everything in my life
And I mean literally everything
Then why give it that chance to do so?
Well, usually it isn't this bad
And I like what he says
And the rush of energy he provides
The clarity that he brings
The fun of being productive and destructive
Is something I didn't know I was craving until he showed up

He's every superhero I've wanted to be
Every main character I've longed to live
His life is pure adventure
And damn if he doesn't have a way with words
I know getting out of that car is a mistake
But I like it when he drives
He shows me what I've been missing from my life
Blasts away this monotonous dreary of mine
He's also the one making most of the decisions
And in his infinite wisdom he knows we'll be fine
Riiiiight up until I'm caught by my partner of nearly a decade
In stolen underwear texting a mutual friend
Jerking off to her bikini pics
And acting as though I don't care if we actually break up
Even though regular me cares
God, does he care
But my friend has his arm around me
Comfortingly telling me I'll be okay
That she's the reason why I'm bored
And that bikini pic friend has invited me out for a catch up
So I know it's meant to be
Where long term is next week
And I'll be out of here come tomorrow
Moving on with life

And enjoying what I've always wanted
So live a little
And don't worry
Because he knows a place where we can both escape this mess
It's easy
I have the car
And he has the keys

THEY'RE ALWAYS INSIDE ME

A lot of lines from songs are still inside me
Gently firing away
More profound than before
A lifeline I needed at that moment
Some ignited after hearing them a dozen times
Heard but not quite ready to be felt
Like working a job I despised
Two years in
Only to hear that just one more year and then you'd be happy
When I had been miserable there all along
That I was a lost soul swimming in a fish bowl
And I cracked
Hid in the warehouse bathroom for ten minutes straight
Knowing that I'd still be there
Year after year
Because I needed the money
More than the sanity

Then I was on my own
Penniless and trying to make it
Longing for someone to show me a way to get out of there
Begging, please won't someone say I'll get out of here

Looking over at my partner
During a rough time for both of us
Wondering if I'd be saying
So long old friend
That I never meant to treat you so badly
To laying my head on the desk
Playing an endless run of somber songs
Turning my world to black
Tattooed all I see

Some fire me up
Others bring me down
Either way they're all in here
Like old friends hanging out
Burning through my soul
Bringing me back in time
My heart melting whenever I hear them play

DEAR PAST SELF

Dear past self
I need you to help me
I need you to change
I need you to find that reason to grab onto something new
And I need you to find it soon
You don't have all the time in the world to correct these habits
And the damage is already building
You don't know it yet but the crash is coming
When life demonstrates how mortal you actually are
You won't be able to choose how it happens
Or even when
But the when and how is fast on its way
And you need to find that reason to change right now
It's hard to make that decision
Harder still to follow through with it
And maybe you're waiting
For life to make that decision for you
Giving you the ultimatum that some receive
But others fail to hear in time
I'm telling you now
It's easier to make that choice today
Taking those baby steps to reclaiming your life
Because at least then you're in control
Able to do it because you wanted to

Instead of weakened by someone else telling you to
So my dearest self
I need you to find that reason
And I need you to find it soon

I REALLY SHOULD

I should stretch when I get out of bed
Wake myself up with some light yoga
Instead of dynamite-level caffeine

I should put the laundry away
Instead of leaving it
Until I wonder where all my clothes have gone

I should have a salad with some grilled chicken
Instead of ordering a pizza like I do every week

I should get some fresh air every day
Instead of putting it off because I just want to sit on the sofa
And stare at a screen

I should knock something off my to-do list
Because it's now the size of a to-do tome

I should spend more time with people I care about
Instead of reading inflammatory comments online
By people I'll never meet

I should spend an hour before bed quietly reading a book
Instead of hoping the next link will entertain me

I should
I might
But I probably won't

I WISH YOU COULD SEE THROUGH MY EYES

I wish you could see through my eyes
So I could show you how far you've come
That the troubling days plaguing you now
Are far in the past and you survived them all

I'd want to point out all the seemingly insignificant days
That became moments of absolute wonder
I'd show you the wild ride still ahead
If only to show you that I don't remember the bad
Nearly as much as I remember the good

If you could see through my eyes
You might wonder how we ever got here
All the things you have to do
All the risks you had to take
And while true, they're also all the things you get to do
A challenge you are capable of

I'm here looking back at you
Hoping that you've reached one of those significant days
So that one day soon
You'll be standing in front of a mirror and it will click
The me of the future
Is you right now

FUTURE ME

It's a strange thing knowing that future me
Is looking through my eyes right now in his memories
He knows something is about to change
Yet I don't know what it is
He knows that insignificant date on my calendar
Will end up being one I talk about for years
He knows the mistakes I'm going to make
The ones I will kick myself over time and time again
Yet they're the ones that changed something about me
Turning me into him
He will recall the unusualness of the days that changed him
The rush of realizing that he had pulled some magical trigger
And that his life had now veered onto a new course
It's curious how he envies my ability to change his past
How I can do all the things he wishes he could've done
And how the journey
Is much more important than the destination
It's a strange thing indeed

THE RUSSIAN

In the space of an hour I fell completely in love with you
From learning your name to seeing our future together
Brought to this place like divine intervention
In an apartment block three stories up
In central Madrid on one trivial summer's day
You were a world traveler, like me
Looking for life, love, and adventure, just like me
Russian, yet from all over the world
To me now living in my fifth country
I wrote books every day
And found you gushing over an author
Who wrote murder mysteries just for his wife
Pulling apart all of the tropes and cliches
And writing it solely for her
Like I would do for you, my love
We exchanged books and life stories
Made coffee and drank wine
You showed me around town on my first day there
And had the most enchanting smile I had ever seen
You were euphoria
The one I had always been searching for
And our life together had just began
Thousands of miles from home
On one trivial day in Spain

It's been fifteen years since I saw you last
And the intoxication of travel wore off after just a week
You're now married
Halfway across the world
We haven't talked in those years either
But I do think about you from time to time
Even though our life together would never have worked
We never even danced
Nor remotely kissed
You were gorgeous and enchanting
And maybe we would've been happy together
But the limerence faded
And has given me pause for later in my years
As whenever I meet the new love of my life
I think back to you
Hoping that it could be the real thing
While aware that you were not the first
Nor the last
Yet, you were the lesson that passion can fade quickly
You are the one I think of more than the others
And your smile is still oh so enchanting

MADRID

The ten bedroom apartment
In the middle of Madrid was a disaster
But it came with all the best stories
A cramped kitchen where we all piled in
Drinking and cooking and telling stories of the world
Twelve of us moving about
From all walks of life
I, the only native English speaker
Yet the bastards conversing as well as me
There was no elevator to help us up those stairs
And we couldn't figure out how
To get into the courtyard down below
Fiestas ran into the street
And the building across the way
Was being demolished every day at five a.m.
Then silence for siesta
And back at it again until dusk
The two sofas could only sit five
And the washing machine rattled so loud
We thought it was going to explode
The whole place was a heat trap
In that blistering summer wave
Where we walked around in a thick layer of sweat every day
Hanging out in the French guy's room

For he had the only working air con
Gambling on when to use the shower
In a bathroom with no lock on the door
And eleven others barging in whenever they liked
We had a household dinner night every week
With a mountain of food and stories shared
Wondering what the three French teenagers were up to
For they were surely just sixteen
With two of them trying to get it on with the third
And all of them living large with no parental supervision
It was a two minute walk to Sol
Or five to the clubs in the north
Getting grinded on by guys and girls alike
My arm around the Swiss girl as I bought her a drink
Striking out then meeting the Italians from class
Then showing them around like I was a seasoned pro
And settling into the tapas bar barely eight feet across
Before moving on to churros con chocolate at four a.m.
And getting six hours of sleep before it all started again
Every day I passed the row of ladies
Perched against the wall of my building
Calling me guapo whenever I strolled by
Saw the museums with the German and Polish girls
Ordered another bottle of wine with the Dutch guy and crew

Watched the Italian flirt with the hot Russian
And the Turk admitting he was not a very good Muslim
As he cracked open another beer
The heat made it impossible to sleep
So we lounged around in a daze
Eventually passing out
With the days and nights blurring together
Until we said farewell to the tenant on their way out
And greeting the overwhelmed one on their way in
They have no idea how weird that place is going to be
Or that there really are only two fridges for twelve people
About to find out that you're able
To look into most people's room from across the courtyard
That group dinner night is going to kick ass
And everyone there knows the weirdest of clubs
The tucked-away bars oozing with locals
Or the perfect place to learn how to salsa
No one ever has any idea of what is happening
So you just roll with it
With the longest of long term here for just three months
While the shortest booked in for ten days
Plenty of time to make a best friend
And life slowly changing before your eyes
I wonder who took over my room when I left

And how different your stories are to mine
It would be wild if I met you one day
But mostly I want to know
What happened to all the friends I never saw again

YOU'RE A WEIRD CAT

You're a weird cat
It's just a doorway, stop being so scared of it
Stop looking at me like I'm going to carry you everywhere
You can do it
And stop jumping at the sight of your own tail
Stop running like hell whenever the toilet flushes
Especially stop rolling around in the wet grass
Then coming back inside to sleep on the sofa
Learn to leave my office door alone
And learn that when I say, "What?"
It means you can stop meowing
And lead me to what you want
Stop drinking the water on my bedside table
Definitely stop throwing up on the rug
When the hardwood floor is just over there
Stop digging your nails into my leg when you stretch
Stop taking up the entire bed
And stop giving me the evil eyes
When I move your fuzzy butt from my face
Or when you try to sit on my keyboard
Just stop
Except don't
Because I love you
You little weirdo

LOVE
ROMANCE
AND ALL THE THINGS IN BETWEEN

YOUR COMFIES

I adore you in your lazy day comfies
Your pajama bottoms kicking at your heels
Your oversized t-shirt halfway down your hips
Yesterday's bra tossed to the side of the room

There is something incredibly sexy about how comfy you look
The feel of your pajamas along your thigh
My hand on your tummy as you lie on the sofa next to me
The bear hugs at your command

It's a look few others will ever see
No longer worried about what I will think
As you are completely relaxed
And there is nothing else we have to do today

THE FIRST SPARK

I remember the moment that spark first ignited
And I wonder when it first sparked for you
You went from unusual to simply extraordinary
And all it took was a reaction from you
And a few simple words
Words of great significance at the time
Though mundane to everyone else
You became my favorite
And the light erupted
I longed to hear from you again
Though I did not know why
You became the reason I had a favorite day
Though I still did not know why
We laughed and clicked
And still I did not know why
Until one day I realized I lingered
And I realized who you were to me
I found myself close enough to reach for you
Afraid I was seeing something that wasn't there
Then our fingers met
Locked in electric intoxication
And the thrill of it all kicked in
A day has not passed since when I have not thought of you
Longed to see you or be with you

From a forbidden kiss to full blown love

A euphoria of knowing what you can do to me

I cherish every moment and every day

To finally being here with you

And seeing you in my heart

I wish we had met years ago

In a different light

In a different world

When things were less complicated

We would've kissed

And we would never have stopped

IF I COULD

If I could slip into your unconscious mind
I would hide the triggers of your spiraling doom
And replace them
With memories of kittens stretching and yawning

I would set up mirrors to all of your fearless moments
So you can see how awesome you are
No matter which dark corner you try to hide in

I'd move the jukebox in your mind
Closer to the tip of your tongue
So you're not stuck on that one lyric all day long
Without knowing who it's by

I would sneak a picture of me into your favorite song
So you remember me smiling at you whenever it plays

I'd light some incense
And find the memory of when we first kissed
So the smell brings you back to that moment
Whenever you need it the most

I would make a note on that mental chalkboard
To keep your keys in the same place every day
So you don't keep losing them like you do

I'd leave silly drawings for you to find
Tucked away in some far-off place
So that you randomly burst out in laughter
Like the goofball I know you are

I would wrap my arms around all of your doubts and fears
So that even in the gloom you know you are loved

I'd cast a brighter light over our first night
So we could see all the details we missed the first time

I would dim the people who annoy you the most
So the ones who bring you joy shine just that much brighter

Most of all
I would show you all the people who are grateful to know you
Because it isn't easy to see what you mean to others
But you mean the world to me
And I'm honored that you have let me in

TOTALLY DIDN'T MEAN TO

Crashing into each other
Music playing
Wine flowing
In a kitchen alive on an electric day
Cheeky laughter bursting from us
And gasps of feigned indignation
As we bump, shuffle and sway
Did I just squeeze your ass?
Totally didn't mean to
Did I just kiss your neck while you were at the stove?
Totally didn't mean to
Did you just drink some of my wine?
Yeah, you totally didn't mean to
Did you just slap my butt
While I'm trying to find the next song to play?
Yeah, you totally didn't mean to
We glide around the room
Aghast that we're onto another bottle
Searching for that track from our teen years
And striking a pose the moment it comes on
Stumbling over the lyrics
And jealous that you saw these guys live
Did we collapse on the floor in complete hysterics?
Yeah, we totally didn't mean to

Did I blow a raspberry on your tummy?
Totally didn't mean to
Did I lose a bet over who sung what song?
Definitely didn't mean to
Did I fall madly in love with you that day?
Totally didn't mean to

EASING INTO THE WATER

Easing into the water
Down to your knees
Smiling across from me
As the bubbles pop and sing
Candles flickering
The wine near
Sandalwood lit
And ash falling below
Steam rises around us
As you sink to your neck
Exhale deeply
And find my hands rubbing your feet
Your eyes fall heavy
Drifting away
Murmuring
Before you lean up
Swivel around
Press your back to my chest
Lay your head against my shoulder
My hands around your waist
My jaw leaning in against your head
Murmuring
Stay with me
Forever in this moment

Just stay
With me

THE MEMORIES OF YOU

I cannot count the memories of you I go to
For they are far too many
The moment our fingers met, certainly
Our lips touching for the first time, definitely
The quiet conversations along the way
As we fell for each other
The birth of in-jokes and regretting the ones that stuck
Whispering, "I love you," and afraid of not hearing it back
Seeing you in your goofy pajamas for the first time
Then wrapped in a towel as you hurry away
To finding all the secret messages you leave for me
And your hungry eyes as you pull me closer
An old favorite bursts from the past
And I wonder how I let it go
Then a new one settles in
And it's like you are embracing me once again
I retreat into them when I seek safety
I go to them when I need to see you
I find the entirety of life within them
And I can't wait to see what more we create
In the years to come

YOU'RE ALWAYS THERE

You're always there
In my heart
My mind
My soul
Smiling at me when I need it
Guiding me when I need a second opinion
Annoying me when I know you're right
Allowing me to vent about so much bullshit
Enjoying you as you agree with all the wrongs in the world
You are my friend
The one I'm in love with
The one who gets me
Who laughs at all the weird things I say
And mocks me when I'm being dumb
I especially think it's cute
Because you are just as mentally ill
Impulsive and amused by silly things
As I am

NOWHERE ELSE TO BE

Sharing a bottle of bubbles
Within the bubbles
As you lean back
Your foot on my lap
My thumb massaging your sole
The soft candlelight nearby
The stars twinkling through the skylight
A gentle fire warming the cabin
Nowhere else to be
Just you and me
We kiss
Unwind
And amid the gentle breeze
We head out onto the veranda
Surrounded by nature
The droplets and suds splashing below
The chill of air
Against our cooling bodies
We kiss again
And make love right there
Just you and me
With no one else around
And nowhere else to be

EVERYWHERE

We kissed on the floor
We kissed all over the sofa
We kissed is the shower
The bath, the great outdoors
Against the setting sun
And surrounded by others going about their day
But the hardest one of all
Was saying farewell as we had to part
Not knowing when we would be together again
If we would ever be together again
With our hearts holding their breath
On the verge of breaking
As we returned to our own lives
Apart
With only these memories to keep us alive

KISS ME

I want you to kiss me here
and here
and here

I want to kiss you there
and there
and there

I want your hands across my body
And mine across yours
As we embrace in mutual bliss

I want you to collapse on top of me
Moaning into my ear
I want to see you vulnerable
And being comfortable with your own fear

I want you to bite your lip
And let me discover what you like
I want you to have your way with me
As I will certainly with you

I want to be so consumed with desire
That we don't even make it to the bedroom

I want you in the middle of the night
With your body wrapped around mine

I want you to kiss me here
and here
and here

And if you show me this right now
I will kiss you there
and there
and there

WITH SOMEONE ELSE

Why is it a thrill to see you with someone else?
His hand on your thigh as you smile
A coy look whenever he gives your leg a squeeze
Before you flick your eyes to meet mine
Breathing in deep then biting your lip
He leans to kiss your cheek
As you twirl the stem between your fingers
He slides his hand up a little higher
And you angle your chin to the side
Letting him kiss you again
Still breathing deep
While watching me

Whatever he whispered in your ear
Has caused you to smile
So he whispers again
And once more your teeth ensnare your lower lip
You drop your hand to his thigh
Trailing your fingertips up his leg
Watching me as you tease us both

He offers to buy you another drink
You flick your eyes back to mine
Is this okay?

Of course
As far as last time?
Further if you like
You look back to him
As I wonder how far you want to go
Now with your hand on his thigh

CRAVE

I crave your touch
Your lips grazing across my skin
Your breath warming my chest
The smell of your hair when I wrap my arms around you

I crave your look
When you know I am yours
Your smile as you feel it too
And your slow blink as you breathe us in

I crave your body against mine
Our clothes tossed to the floor
The whisper just for me
Holding each other closer and closer still

I crave to be with you every day
Together like we should be
Your soul at ease
As mine is with you

IT'S ALWAYS YOU

On the sofa
Curled up beside me
Sharing a blanket
As the fat tropical rain splatters against the window
Thumping the tin roof like a chorus of gentle hammers
My fingers rubbing your head
Watching the embers in the fire smoldering brightly
Talking random shit until you burst out laughing
Then smile at me like I'm an idiot
You settle back under my arm
Squeezing me tightly
Your soul at peace
I love you
I love you too
You close your eyes
Capturing this moment for later
Holding onto it for when we are far apart
Asking me what I'm thinking about
And the answer is simple enough
You
It's always you
And I love you for that

THE DANCE

The music hums as you back away
Your hands gliding through your hair
Hips sashaying from side to side
As though I'm melting in your hands
Your fingers reach your buckle
Gently freeing the little catch
Tugging at your top
And slowly spinning around
You peel your trousers down an inch
Your tee exposing your belly
Lifting it free
Over your shoulders and into your hand
As you rhetorically ask if I would like more
You spin again
Glancing over your shoulder
With a gentle bite of you lip
Of course I want more
I want it all
And you drop your tee into my lap
Slowly lean forward
And slide your trousers to your ankles
Your hand reaching to my shoulder for balance
Then straddling me as you tease with a kiss
Breathe into my ear as my hands caress your body

You slap them away
Biting your lip
Not yet, you say
And turn again
Leaning back against my chest
Your head on my shoulder
Your hands gliding up to my hair
Mine working their way across your body
Until you sit forward
Shake your back
Highlighting the clasp
Help me with this, you say
And soon your hand pins it to your chest
For an eternity of near reveals
As you shimmy
Sashay
And tease me constantly
You come forward again
Press your chest against mine
Release your hands
Wrap them around my head
Your bra now free
As you bury my face into your chest
And feel my gentle kiss

You rhetorically ask if I would like more
Before you stand again
Come hither me forward
I fall to my knees
With your body gliding from side to side
Your hands working their way up
As you whisper softly
Are you at my mercy?
Good
Now take them off me

I SHOULD'VE MET YOU YEARS AGO

I should've met you years ago
Even though it was wholly impossible
The world was a different place
And we were so far apart
Unable to be
Not even ready
But believe me
I was looking for you
Not someone like you
But you

There is a world where we never met
One where we're still searching
I ache for them
Wonder who they became
And why it had to be
So the next time I see you
The next time we kiss
It'll be with the weight of all those worlds
Making up for how they never met

YOUR MOVE, MY DEAR

My hand against the small of your back
The other cradling your head
Swaying with the music
Your face nestled against my chest
The contours of your dress
The ridges in the fabric inviting
As I slide my hand down
Making a move
And with lightning speed
You swat my palm away
Still calm and smiling against my chest
As though it was merely a fly
You breathe in
At peace with the evening
My hand still stings
And we sway
The music pulling us away
I reach for your side
You slap my back with a quick up-flick
Stinging me though my shirt
Then you breathe in with satisfaction
Gently sigh as you look the other way
And nuzzle deeper into my chest
In a perfect calm

As the music settles once again
I go for your rear
Lift my hand quickly as you snap a third strike
Striking yourself with lightning speed
Your eyes jolt awake
Startled with betrayal
While I grin
Look the other way
Calm and content
And await the revenge that will certainly come my way

OUR FIRST KISS

The stars exploded
The moon soared
And the quiet of the night careened off a cliff
The moment you laid your arm around my waist
Looking to me with nervous eyes
A longing within your gaze
The restless tiger pounding inside
Consuming me whole
Your hand squeezed a little tighter
Hoping that you weren't out of line
I leaned in
Pressed my lips against yours
Frantic and passionate
Unable to get enough of you
And you were everything I wanted
As I tore at you
You biting me in return
Unable to break away
Refusing to retreat
And it was not enough
Nowhere near enough
Yet here I stand
Facing the twinkling stars
The falling moon

The gentle evening breeze
With you absent from my side
Mulling over the passion
Hoping to see you again
Terrified that I won't

INTO THE MADNESS

Into the madness I fall
To my knees
To your feet
For your touch
Breathing deep
All these moments
Until I see you again

Running through my mind
Hoping to find
Some way to make you smile
If normal is madness
Then here comes ecstasy
As you crest over the hill
And come to me
Tell me why
Am I so mad about you?
So crazy for you

Into the madness I fall
Hoping to see
A way for me
And you to be
Counting all the ways

We could be free
Yet here I am
Losing my mind
Losing sleep
And can't unwind
Can't wait
Can't stop
Can't sit still
Until I'm with you again
Tell me why
Am I so crazy for you?
So mad about you

Into the madness I fall
Obsessed with you
Drunk on you
In love with you
And still I lose my mind
That you are the purpose in my life

Why am I so mad about you?
So crazy for you

ONE DAY

The door closes and I push you against the wall
Kiss you frantically as your arms lock around me
Move to your neck as you tear off my belt
I drop to my knees and lift your skirt
Your fingers curling through my hair
Begging me not to stop
You pull me up and push me back
Eye me carefully as you lower yourself down
The warmth enraptures me and I can't take it anymore
I lift you onto the dining table
Still trying to peel the layers away
We kiss
Embrace
Passions flare
And fireworks burst
As though we're running out of time
I've wanted you for so long
You've wanted me
Unable to keep our hands off each other
With no perfect time except for the time we have right now
And now we're finally here
Collapsing together
Breathing deep
Words failing

And we kiss
Whispering each other's name
Muttering, 'holy shit'
One day we might make it to the bedroom
One day
Though last time we barely made it past the front door

SOMETIMES THERE'S NOTHING TO FIX

Sometimes there's nothing anyone can do in these situations
There's nothing to fix
It's just something you have to ride through
And though it may be unbearable at times
And you want to give up completely
I am here for you to lean on
And I will keep you company

I THINK OF YOU ALL THE TIME

I think of you all the time
Even when I'm dreaming, you're there
When I wake up, you're on my mind
When I go to bed, I whisper to you
Even when you're miles away
When I'm having a bad moment, the mere thought of you
Warms my soul
When I'm anxious
A hug from you helps more than you know
When you laugh, I melt
When you cry, I burst
When you tell me you love me, I fall
When you say you think of me all the time, I know
And when I tell you you're the best part of my day, believe me
It's true

REMEMBER HOW WE DANCED?

Remember how we danced together?
The first time our hands met
The slow entwining
Fingers curling
Spark forming
Danger rising
It wasn't enough
Nowhere near enough
Then we found each other again
After all those months had passed
As though we always should have been
As though we always will
We dance again
Your head against my chest
My hand stroking your hair
Your arms curled around me
Now with magic in the air
The touch of my suit
The feel of your dress
It's no longer a spark
But an inferno under duress
The clink of wine glasses
And food warming our souls
Under the dim amber lights

Near the coastal strolls
From the crashing waves
Comes a gentle breeze
The open signs flipped
The night coming to ease
I whisper to you
And you squeeze me tighter
We drift away
The world a little lighter
We spin
We embrace
We dream of a life
While still in this place
It took years to find you
And seconds for our souls to entwine
The start of our life forming
As though the stars really did align
It was just the back of a restaurant
Outside in the dark
But it was that exact space
Where the songbirds from our grandchildren may hark
I remember so much
Yet the details are few
Except for falling

So completely in love with you
It's still a chorus of memories
Brought to such vivid life
From a perfect moment
Within a perfect night

THE MADNESS

I have come to accept the madness we live
And how others caution against it
What tragic lives they must lead
To fear such a life of sin and revelry
Of bliss and freedom
Of the intoxication one person can wring from you
It truly baffles me that others fear what you and I have
While they still search for exactly what we share
A love
A bond
A soul shared
And the acceptance that neither of us are perfect
But maybe we're perfect for each other

I'M GLAD I MET YOU

I'm glad I met you
With every ounce of my soul
And beat of my heart
I'm glad I met you
You challenge me in ways I never dreamed of
Yet always hoped to find
You're annoyingly good at things I'm already good at
And you're always on my mind
You are wise and sensible
Cunning and electric
Passionate and soulful
Intoxicating and gorgeous
Daring and brave
While vulnerable and afraid
You have awakened something deep inside
And I love that I have awakened it in you as well
Somehow I didn't feel empty before you
But as soon as you came along something clicked into place
Like you should have always been there
Yet were always with me
Twin flames finding each other
As we realized the impact of it all
There's a reason it's you
And there's a reason it's me

You inspire me
And enfire me
You drop my jaw to the ground
And I still beg for more
You promise me no promises
And I promise to aspire you more
To awaken you further
And to be with you when you do
So you become more cunning and electric
More daring and brave
More devious and sinful
Because with every ounce of me I want you
And with every ounce of you
You want me too

IT DOESN'T JUST DISAPPEAR

Love like this doesn't just disappear
It doesn't run away when shit gets real
It doesn't judge
It just accepts
It holds you when you need it the most
It has your back when you are scared
It offers you a hand when you have fallen
It reassures you when you are in doubt
So believe me, my love
Though you may still be scared
Still have fallen
Still harbor some fear
I've got you
And you have no need to question that

WE FELL SO EASILY

We fell into each other so easily
That I have to pinch myself in case you're not real
Then I hold you
And I fall even further
So I want to thank you
For falling with me
I hope one day you'll be in bed
Lying back while reading this
Knowing it's just for you
Debating which page is your favorite
Maybe I'll be beside you
Maybe I won't
Either way, it's okay to pinch me
And then kiss me
Whisper my name
So I may fall a little further

HEARTACHE

WE DIED A LITTLE

We died a little over the years
Running out of new stories and repeating the old
Bickering after a few too many
Disappointed by the constant stress of money
Playing all the new games until we've grown tired
Watching shows with glee until they no longer enthral
Penciling in date night
Instead of it being a given
Yet never have anything to talk about
So we figure out what to watch instead
As though our lives are perpetually on standby
We try again the following week
But you have to work late
Because some idiot got overwhelmed
And punted their job onto you
Full of mistakes you have to fix
As someone vents to you and you vent to me
While I apologize for the uninspiring dinner
Without music or life or spice to enliven us
As I went through the routine of chopping and stirring
Clock-watching as ten o'clock looms ahead
Instead of throwing caution into the wind
And staying up past midnight like we used to
Captured in the passion of our early days

Before the limerence faded

And we became ... this

Maybe we'll get it right next time

Or the one after

Even though I can't do next week

And we have that thing we can't get out of the week after

We definitely need to liven things up

Though we still haven't found another couple to befriend

And our reliable pair have just broken up

Now curious as to what drove them apart

Was it infidelity?

Was it suffocating standards and failure to live up to them?

Maybe they simply ran out of things to say

So we compare

Reading between the lines

Their writing on the wall

Looking a lot like ours

An awful lot like ours

But that's them

Definitely not us

Only ... when did sex stop being fun?

Why are we having to schedule it

Instead of tearing at each other's clothes like we used to?

A single drink and our clothes were on the floor

Now we slump on the sofa trying to watch something new
Finding excuses to remain busy
Instead of excuses to be with each other
There are no longer passionate kisses
Simply a perfunctory greeting in the morn
I notice everyone else as they walk by
Instead of the smile you have just for me
How long has it been since we had it all?
How long since we were the envy of others?
How long do we still have left?
Have we reached our point of no return?
I don't know how we started dying
I just hope we haven't died completely

OUR LITTLE GIRL

Do you remember her name?
Our little girl who never was?
She never breathed a single breath
Never had a beating heart
But man, does she still live
The cutest little thing
Clutching my finger with all of hers
Holding our hands as we swing her down the street
Stomping in her big girl boots
Thick coat
And woolly hat
Showing off her crayon picture of a cat
And okay, it's not great
But we tell her it is
And put it on the fridge next to menus of takeout
Until we realize it's one of the things we'd save in a fire
Long drives with her fast asleep in the back
Carrying her up to bed after movie night
Playing games every weekend
With ever-increasingly complex rules
Until she starts to come up with them herself
And dear God we've given birth to a rules lawyer
What have we done?
She has my eyes

Your smile

Our brains

But she's not as smart as she thinks she is

Though she is quickly gaining on us

Grade six and we're held hostage at a school play

The chorus are struggling to find the same key

But at least the costume we spent all night working on is on point

And her diction is impeccable

Ivy league here we come

Oh God, ivy league?

That shit's going to be expensive

Just as long as she doesn't become an English major

If she does she can spend four years 'studying' somewhere cheaper

Now she needs braces

And she thinks she looks hideous

But they'll be gone in a year and a half

Now there's something called a training bra?

Why?

What exactly are they training?

You whisper to me that she confessed

To kissing someone else for the first time

And I'm mortified to realize I don't know the kid we're talking about

Though not as mortified when I can no longer distinguish my wife's expensive underwear from my daughter's

Asked to the prom
And I really have to judge her fashion sense
Because that choice certainly didn't come from me
Now she's out late
Too late
And I know she'll be fine
I know she'll be fine
I know she'll be ...
Oh thank fuck, that's her coming in through the front door
Oh
She had a fight
And broke up
Tells me she doesn't need me right now
And I ache
I don't know what to do
She's in agony and just wants to be alone
The little girl I used to push in swings
The one who melted at seeing a puppy for the first time
She's in agony and there's nothing I can do
I know she'll be okay because I went through this before
But this was her first true love
That leaves a mark
Mine certainly did
And she's no longer being as open

I have to figure everything out from little clues

Which go on a merry-go-round of contradiction every damn day

She no longer rides in the back but the front of the car

Asks to borrow the keys when everything on the road is trying to her

My heart cracks as I tell her to please be careful out there

Because if she doesn't come home ...

We're about to move house again

And there's a shoebox full of things on the top shelf in the closet

A drawing of an oddball cat in crayon whose name I still remember

The bracelet she wore at hospital when we first took her home

A picture of our first Christmas when it was snowing

Her letter from camp

You put the picture of the cat back on the fridge

And I lose control

I want those moments back

I want to live them again for the first time

Because now she's gone

Her hand clutching mine

She's gone

Her laughing in a swing

She's gone

Her climbing into our bed with Billy the Rabbit

She's gone

The name you chose for her

The one I knew was perfect the moment I heard it
Our little girl is gone

We got a pill
Better safe than sorry, I suppose
But even so she was real
Had a whole life we could see
A magical one
I miss her
Every fucking day I miss her
Our little girl

I CAN'T

I wish I could live with your forever
But I can't
What we have would become life
Of chores and a loss of romance
Of dead bedrooms
And appointments to keep
Of knocking down this wall
To create a better flow
Of paint swatches
And over priced quotes
Of bemoaning the idiots at work
And the fools on the road
Slipping into comfies at the end of the day
Instead of dressing up to impress you
Watching TV with a meal on our laps
Instead of at the table as we fall in love
Of existing without living
Of fights and grievances building
As we both fail each other's expectations
Compared to who we presented when we first kissed
We will disappear into tiredness
Uninspiring routine
And a life mundane
I love you

I wish I could have this moment forever
But I can't

DON'T FALL IN LOVE WITH SOMEONE LIKE ME

Don't fall in love with someone like me
I will confide in you
See you as you really are
Remember things about you that no one else does
Challenge you to go after your dreams
Be the reminder that you can do this
Get how your mind works
Laugh at both of our expense
Because you're my kind of weirdo
One of the rare few in the world
Whose heart beats in time with mine
Slowly I will fall in love with you
But you should never fall in love with me
I will write my way into your heart
Tease you with food I have prepared
Be one of the few to wish you a happy birthday without a reminder
Send you random messages because I think you'll find them funny
Think of you when you're not around
But you should never fall in love with me
I will share my romantic dreams
My ideals of a perfect life
Reach for your hand when no one else is looking
And feel that electric energy rush between us

I will kiss you with a passion you've always longed for

Be the story you dreamed of living

Travel a world of fantasy with you

Then live reality the way we must

I will let your mind rest as I do the dishes

Clean up after us both

Take the dog out for a walk

Then do a shopping run so you can lounge on the sofa

Watching trashy movies to your heart's content

I will do my fair share of the chores instead of expecting you to do them all

And tell you every day how much I love you

But you should never fall in love with me

We will live together

Travel the world

Chase our dreams

And entwine our lives so thoroughly that we can never be undone

I will make you French toast every Sunday

Rub your feet when you ask for it

And hope you sleep well every night

But you should never fall in love with me

Because I have never entered a relationship without an exit plan

I fall only for the complicated

I fall if you are leaving the country

Adore you if you are already married

Fantasize over you even when our boss is watching

And even though I hate it with every ounce of my soul

I hate that I lie because of self preservation

That despite being so thoroughly in love with you

You are not the one I'm going to spend the rest of my life with

And I've known that since day one

THANK YOU FOR READING

Want to read more? Check out Lost in the Bookshelf.

ACKNOWLEDGMENTS

I am lucky enough to know some wonderful people who put aside time in their hectic lives to not only read the things I write but who also give me feedback on poems I have written about them. As you might imagine this can be fraught with tension, yet they are generous enough to read what I send them with an analytical eye instead of a bruised ego. Even more surprising is that none of them have yet to say, "Please don't publish this one about me."

So, a thousand thank yous to Alesandra, Vanessa, and Laura.

Also a big thank you to you, the reader. I'm sure you've got things to do and yet you took the time to read this. So, cheers.

ABOUT THE AUTHOR

Stefano spends his days in front of a computer with questionable posture while genuinely forgetting about the never-ending to do list that never gets done. He has two fuzzballs who keep the house safe from mice. He hails from Australia.

Made in the USA
Columbia, SC
25 September 2022

67929011R00074